The Explosion of Binary Stars

The Explosion
of Binary Stars

Debby Jo Blank

Shearsman Books

First published in the United Kingdom in 2012 by
Shearsman Books
50 Westons Hill Drive
Emersons Green
Bristol
BS16 7DF

Shearsman Books Ltd Registered Office
30–31 St. James Place, Mangotsfield, Bristol BS16 9JB
(this address not for correspondence)

http://www.shearsman.com/

ISBN 978-1-84861-197-9

Contents

This book is dedicated to my brother,
Andy Blank, 1957–2010

Andy & Debby Jo Blank, 1992.

An Air France Flight from Rio to Paris

When the bird went down we could not see it
break into silver reflections that careened
off the skin of deep waters, hear it explode
into the silence off Fernando de Noronha
where men catch aerodynamic dog snapper
with scoop nets they mend over and over.
If there was lightning, we didn't see it.
Maybe the storm clouds were like walls
as massive as the walls of Jericho.
Charybdis threatening to swallow them whole—
all those people and one baby, 228,
not a lottery ticket or the molecular weight
of gold—196.97, if you care.

The next time I climb onto the back
of a bird and sit astride it like a jockey,
my arrows clenched in my teeth,
I will whisper the name of the drowned.
Or maybe I will take a pill, wear my best
underwear and imagine pages of my diary
afloat atop the salt water, all the different colored
inks smudged, my words running
together until what's left looks
like a Rothko water color of sea anemones.
Yes, of course, the diaphanous tutus
of sea anemones amid the debris.

Under the Snow

After dinner I scrounge for my ticket
to give to the underground parking attendant
whose cuffs of his bulky hand-knit sweater
are pulled low over his hands.
Inside his glass cubicle a book of physics
lies open, I recognize such plutonium
packed pages, the cramped numbers
amid a few "q"s, "x"s, "f"s and "y"s .

A former boyfriend studied Special Problems,
tried to explain the difficulty of rulers
without calibrations small enough to measure
the speed of elementary particles or large enough
to determine the height of a cliff from which a rock
is dropped, if the splash is heard six second later
and sound travels at 340 meters per second.
Over these dilemmas, outside the familiarities
of Euclidean space, he would frown and scribble
tight equations hour after hour, while I streamed
through Faulkner, intoxicated and out of breath
in the green of a single run-on sentence,
page after page dotted with hidden moonshine
stills and the scent of Magnolia trees in bloom.

I query this thirty-some guy with hairy fingers
who has apparently immigrated from the bowels
of Russia with a Green Card, acquired through
the largesse of a philanthropic organization
which helps Jewish scientists come to teach
at Columbia or CalTech, though I discern some
have fallen through the grate like lost keys and toil
as night janitors or parking lot attendants to put milk

on their oil-clothed tables in apartments that smell
of root vegetables and sweat. I hand over $10 and ask
further about his studies—his field of research
is the neutrinos produced in *electron-positron annihilation.*
I think of the fragile bones of Russian ponies
buried beneath the snow of the Volga steppes.

Remembering Three Walled Cemeteries

1. k'riah

In the wall of darkness a tale
Is enshrined like a star

Its mortar tastes like ash

But nothing can be explained in this way—
Explanations make sense
    In the way of explanations only

Things the eye cannot long hold
Expelled on a low tide

2. onen

    We saw them piled by the river
    We try to forget
    But we close our eyes
    And see them by the river
    When we fall asleep

Our river shorn of its blue
Promises nothing, moves too fast to befriend

Friends died together, held out their hands

    The radishes black as spiders
      As if a film of butter lay across his open eyes
        Only a hawk above the potato field
        The school gate rusted off its hinges
          Bricks from the station's chimney toppled across
                        the tracks
        The train tracks no one would bomb

3. *taharah*

Crushed skulls in the dirt—
    Shells in starlight, fragments
    Of men whisper electrical
    Messages between cortical cells
    Gyrations of white matter
    Where dead men live on
    As ghosts amid the matter
    Of fresh bread with seeds
    Soup on the stove
    Fragrant, innocent as a cow

Baby wolves howl
For their mother under
The new moon

The other moon
Also howls

    Carpenters file to the square with wooden bowls
        Butterflies migrate through our eyelashes
            A mouse guards the kitchen door
                Twisted loaves with seeds

When things are this bad, things do not line up
Jelene is gone
Ninita never goes out after dark
Vassi never kisses under the new moon
No one has a cat
No one remembers the name of their cat
We cannot imagine a world with cats

4. k'vurah

The liar always finds some woman
    To love him
    Anyway

A fellowship of liars
    Who took away
    The men
    Turned men into soap
    Turn soap into lead
    What's left by the drain
    What's left before the brain
    Drops
    Into sleep
    At this point in history
    A point has no dimensions
    No perspective

    No eye
    No I

Still they howl
Drops of rain begin to fall

5. kevod ha-met

In the long-padlocked theater
    At last the red curtain rises
    Again above the empty stage
    The audience sits transfixed
    By the playwright back from an island
    Of bananas, parrots and moss

Who writes a permissible play
With the prop of a bowl of cherries
That sits throughout the three acts
A man shaves off his beard
The mystery concerns a miscarriage
Dust to dust
During two interminable intermissions
People smoke on the steps
Above the plaza empty as rain

6. *chesed shel*

Liars with gay batons and ingots
On their soapbox shoulders
The ones who followed orders, too
Somehow them, too

The sounds of leaves keep them awake
Lines of men caught in the music of leaves
Or the dreams of children
Separated from their mothers
What measurement can be salvaged?

Above all, the uniforms must be proper

As, after all, we come from dust

7. *tachrichim*

From the roof you can see the ocean
    A sliver of blue just a bit darker
        An azure crease
            The color of Vassi's eyes

Fingers moves the beads
    Beads the color of ocean

Prayer beads to finger over and over
If we say this over and over, it will still be true

A loaf with seeds no one eats
    Seeds the color of ivory, the color of bones
        Crushed by the waves of rain
        Of years, of ash, of other things
        In orbit behind the eye

Behind the old church of St. Volodymyr
The venerable monk pulls out the bad tooth
Without whiskey, twists his pliers with all his force
Bends his knees for extra torque

    This plaza is where it happened
    They took them away
    The one-armed man with a moustache
    Oversaw their burial
    Like teeth in the furrows of the field
    So many lies cannot hide the truth
    Bodies piled like matches

8. *hevra kadisha*

Jelene cannot forget
A wild bird sick inside her chest
She cannot remember the prayer
Does it go right to left or left to right?
Do they hear it? Is there a stove pipe

Into the heavenly body
To transmit the prayers
The full range of notes
The bass grandfather missing a thumb
The soprano fiancé in her red kerchief
Children off-key in the choir of St. Volodymyr
The old plumber who snores

>Dragons arise from the buried teeth
>The plaza buried in ash

The cat named Lena is gone
For days hunting the meat of the moon
Vassi feeds the hawk with a broken wing
On the plaza old men drink tea in the afternoon
Across the plaza girls walk arm-in-arm
Jelene talks to herself
>The baker feeds her day-old rolls with seeds
For all of these animals and people only three cemeteries!
>Three walled cemeteries

>People buried where they fell

9. *emet*

First Ninita fills her pockets with stones
Then she burns the scrap of paper
The directions take her deep into the forest
A hundred paces to the south her dress rips off like paper
Near the river that is too fast to befriend

No pears ripen here

Bubbles come to the surface
A door blows open
        And slams
        Boom!

Unlit candles kept in the drawer
The moon lengthens each day
Like a teardrop or a boy's
Kite so high it is a red dot
In the overcast sky
No day exactly the same length
Jelene uses her tongue to shine the soupspoon
    A bush bursts into flames

    The faculty thrown from the roof
    The youngest boy escaped
    They bolted the door and set the building on fire

10. *sheloshim*

Fresh wolf tracks in the snow
White candles in the drawer
    An abandoned rat's nest in the tablecloth
        Discolored lace in shreds
            Coming apart
            In the cold center of the moon

She closes her mouth to guard the darkness
A cousin of darkness seeps out of her open eyes
The father of darkness smothers the river inside her
An orphan of darkness naked in the light of her stars
    All these darknesses rule the catacombs of her body
        Inexplicably three cemeteries

Along the Linden Path

That May our destination was Laguiole,
a town of knife makers high on a pastoral plateau
dotted with the cream of cows too beautiful to eat.
Our honeymoon, *la lune de miel*,
the Michelin-starred menu, champagne,
squash blossoms and artichoke buds.

In our knife-edged white room, *N° 10*,
succumbed to beauty, voile curtains open
to the green sea beyond our cocoon of linen
mussed with open mouths, maybe … wings.
Do you know what I mean?

On rutted backways a *XIIe siècle abbaye*
the color of spent blood not well-captured
in the photo, my face lost below the brim
of my floppy hat—so much green at work.

Our stone cottage next to Zebulon's field,
the donkey who begged for apples and brayed
when we approached along the Linden path.
Oh, the affections of this donkey with clouds of flies at his eyes.

Sinewy wine, baguettes and cheeses from Sarlat,
sliced with a picnic knife before the onslaught
of beauty in the iron bed, cold as night sighed
on and Zeb brayed below its far-off lanterns.

Why bother now with this old story,
its blade deep in my chest?
We were binary stars who knew nothing
yet of knife wounds in the light of our first Spring.

The Blue Man

We call him the *Blue Man*—
as if from the moon in his padded blue
space suit, some Homerian creature
shroud in inky leather skin—the spindle cells
of *Kaposi's sarcoma* invade his skin, his lungs,
even his tongue. We talk about him
as we drink coffee before rounds,
having never before seen a blue man.

That sly retrovirus from Cameroon once lived
in peaceful coexistence with chimps until
it jumped to a more vulnerable host—
a prostitute in a batik kerchief, an addict
bitten by a pimp, an accountant from the city
with a fast car—this plague that nothing heals.

The Blue Man rasps as he sucks air into his miserable
sinkhole lungs, I can't maneuver the needle through
his elephantine skin. I try a joke about Interns
weak from lack of sleep, open a second sterile kit
with a blowgun-size needle, but his cyan hide is still
too tough and he's fallen into his last dream.

A Breast Cancer Survivor Named Irma

Once she danced with scarves,
now it's steel cold, so she'll need a fire
to build a ladder into the sky.

For years between thighs that rumble
things that should not have been done,
like the President in office who risks everything
for a girl with big lips who was not even born
when he began to contrive his way
to the granite halls of power.

So many toppled warriors, secrets, chrysalis folded
inside all of us, such pitiful beings.

This is the next-to-last chapter,
the turned back of his silence, how love unstitched
their polite cloth and went cold.

There's nothing left after countless rounds
of chemo, radiation ports tattooed
on her chest. Now, he's come round
asking for what used to be his,
an easy yoke to break.

Nothing she reaches for quite works,
the richness of that syrup
irradiated to chalk, even her eyes,
dry as grackles in the catalpa.

Maybe if he would use his tongue
for once, she could find her way to spring
rams in the curly green, the egg moon,
before it disappears on the wheel of light.

Helena on the Surgical Floor

1.
She wants to talk to you of her body.
Not the beans that filter water,
not the miles of conduits filled
with crushed flowers, and certainly
not the temple with its buzzing ears,
its loading docks heavy with aliquots
of minerals and glandular extrusions.

You know the place of which she speaks
from your travels into the steam of navels
and armpits you've loved, from the time you ran
out of breath beneath the enormous wave
in Zihuatanejo, the years of your whispers
you wanted no one else to hear, least of all yourself.

2.
That was then and this is now.
Was she ever that beautiful?
The surgeons cut out the syncytium,
that tapestry of tissue without name
in the vault where electricity once gathered,
where umber was squeezed out like sweat
after hard work, where the body became
unzipped, knocked senseless, deboned, sated.

3.
She is trying to explain how gold dust
was blown to bits, dissected away,
lost after her hysterectomy—that thrill
in the throat of a warbler high in the sycamore,
that ripple of muscle clenched against itself.

She hates to admit this tundra of absence,
this heath in the chill of early March
when at last the dogs are let out
to run and howl into the face of the moon
who is blind and without urgency.

Beyond Enemy Fire

—at the VA in New Hampshire

Half-dragged in by two guys who dump him
by the desk and disappear back into the night.

A stinking trail of mud, blood and shit on the linoleum
galvanizes Sharon, the charge nurse, to grab

the phone and stat-page the night janitor and Intern
on-call, in that order. Dr. Marks comes down,

smells him before he reaches the cubicle.
Emaciated, prehensile, greasy long hair and beard,

he moans – his 1.4 million year-old flint
nowhere to be found. Sharon cuts away

his ruined clothes—back to his *Homo ergaster* state,
Brian Franklin Hyde, twenty-nine years old,

looks forty. Dr. Marks tries not to gag,
writes his note—PTSD, ETOH, hematochezia,

Normal Saline, Valium, Vancomycin—
on the gurney, Mr. Hyde passes out.

Three days later he's back in the human race,
almost handsome beneath infusion bags,

patched up, ready to find his way back to his cave.
Patty, the social worker, blond hair up in a French twist,

comes by and does her best. But he's sure,
he wants to stay in the woods, prefers his hominid life

beyond enemy fire. He reads the paper
and turns down offers of meds for his nightmares.

Discharged after ten days, he climbs into
a banged up Chevy truck that blares Procol Harum.

He'll be back—reeking, unable to walk upright,
carry stones or speak—back in his caveman disguise.

A Chinese Menu

This poem can be enjoyed on many levels.
If you know the allusions, of course it works
better, but it's not necessary to be familiar
with the reference to Wittgenstein's notion
found in the *Tractatus* that every proposition
is true or false. You can still appreciate what a Zen
koan might make of this rigidity and revel
in the half-full state of the teacup necessary for nirvana,
as tenuous as the disappearance of Pascal's sentient
red balloon in the clouds over the 20ème arrondissement
of Paris or the famous *Problem of the Two Balloons,*
where the greater internal pressure of the smaller
balloon will force air into the larger, even though
this might not be intuitively obvious and requires
knowledge of the radius of curvature and other
such laws of physics, which are apt to be true
if we stick to the world of things governed
by gravity and keep away from the laws that govern
very small things, where time can dilate
and space contract, mechanics as inscrutable
as a married couple's predetermined approach
to a Chinese menu (she'll order for them both,
but take into account his penchant for shrimp
and sensitive stomach) or what happens when
the baby's heart rate decelerates and a c-section
is advised in the U.S. much more frequently than,
say, Denmark, where my taxi driver, originally
from Istanbul, was so insulted by the cartoon
of Mohammad in a diaper turban that I was unsure
how to be polite and not take sides, which brings us
full-circle, back to how Wittgenstein might
have modified his treatise if he'd been able
to have a steak dinner with the Dalai Lama
(who is not a vegetarian).

Amsterdam

Years of hard drinking with Elie, Primo and Jerzy,
their stories tattooed beneath my nails and Celan's
milk cup buried near the twisted Myrtle,
Klemperer whispers of half-finished eggs, Frankl
measures my scapulae to memorialize their wing span.

On a bench by her museum unwilling to stand in line,
as if I escaped that attic, evaded the factories of smoke,
as if swarms of B-17s came to the rescue, as if no one
counted gold fillings, these numbers do not add up!
Too many teeth, too many lampshades,
too many diamonds sewn inside their hems.

Ariel is gone, the tired general with blood in his brain—
as if Sharon's wall could protect us from ourselves.

Our ashes in smoke long after theirs have disappeared
in the skies of Belzec, Chelmno and Najdanek,
as if good deeds count, six million, it's nothing.

Up Prinsengracht again to the church across
from The Anne Frank House, I can't get inside,
my body won't move off the cement bench.

In the hotel a man in a silk suit selects a cigar
from the humidor, fondles several before he decides,
the pale girl in her pert dress hands him a knife
to excise the tip, leaves a box of matches for him
to work, her skirt very short over black tights,
as if his plume carries the molecules of millions.

A handsome couple sprawls in fog on a daybed,
the room's become a tomb, the votive glow

of candles on white tablecloths, napkins like swans,
glassware tinkles, tears crease my palms,
the man with his cigar and the tangled duo.

Once a warehouse for silk and porcelain,
glossy chestnut trees shade its courtyard,
a perfect square with fashionable luggage
carried by the doorman in his sleek black.
A siren blares across the Keizersgracht Brug,
the same sound from newsreels of the war.

My glass is empty, the check is signed,
I climb the steps painted whale, the muted
pattern of mourning, pewter on pewter,
my key on a brass circle engraved "33,"
a number that might mean something,
but doesn't, sleep elusive against frosty
sheets, as if *they're* piled next to me.

Hunkered down again on the bench,
B-17s drone en masse, coming to the rescue,
the Westerkerk peals through her veiled window.

6 Guilders at Jonas Daniel Meijerplein
to view the Chagalls, the restored Cor Hunds,
the altar, *what were the probabilities?*
The building's four synagogues renovated
inside a shell of glass and steel, remnants
of the meat market below the Obbene Shul.

Ducks in formation and boats, the smell of diesel
dies in their wakes, even the crickets sound aghast.

How can they bring children? The bell strikes,
sixty-four years since she wrote, *Dear Kitty*.

Bygones are bygones in tolerant Amsterdam.
An Albanian garbage collector in a jump-suit
sweeps near the wall, bricks made in kilns.
A blind woman holds out a lock of hair,
my great-grandfather sweeps the courtyard,
the sun hidden in the restraint of Dutch clouds.
On the bench with Van Gogh, Rembrandt,
kanaals, bicycles, tulips, my legs heavy as cement.

Somewhere Near the Mediterranean

The town we yearn to stroll through—
wide marble steps the color of doves,
hidden cobblestone squares with fountains
where small boys dart with a ball,
cats atop pillars in the sun,
crumbling balconies with flowerpots
and everywhere ochre walls, the full spectrum
of ochres, flaxen to mustard—
       this town we yearn for no longer exists.

We drive into this yearned-for town, park
our rented mini-car, without the convenience
of automatic shift, in a blacktop lot
where a machine disgorges tickets
to be paid in Euros (exact change only),
bands of tourists recite from guidebooks,
shop for memorabilia in the little stands
that overflow onto sidewalks—
       this is not the town we meant to visit.

Maybe if we walk further, we will find it—
the park with statues of minor dignitaries,
new mothers who fuss with prams, an old woman
in black with her satchel who waves hello,
house numbers painted on blue-and-white tiles,
familiar stray dogs who nuzzle us
in air of mint and sage polished by the sun,
a gold our camera cannot capture—
       this is the town we cannot find.

We sign bills for expensive meals that do not
meet our expectations, sleep with our shutters

closed to the gang on scooters below,
over-tip at cafes, struggle with maps
to locate parking near museums (no flash allowed),
but, alas, although we came in May—
we find only the crowds we'd hoped to avoid.

No One Saw Me Close Your Eyes

I can watch over you better up there,

placed for safekeeping in the third star

of the handle as light erases the Big Dipper.

Pistons, crank shafts or torque, who cares

about internal combustion, all the things

you don't need to understand to drive?

At its tipping point, unable to assemble bile,

retire worn out hemoglobin, the burden

of your tumor trespasses your liver.

Things are beyond *rage, rage,*

spent oxygen, hydrogen, carbon of your last exhalation

disperse in dark matter beyond the reach of my arms.

Your electricity fires the engines of stars, steers starfish

off Patagonia, stirs the currents of Madagascar.

Horses in Hana

The distant waves are Hawaiian drums,
white birds settle and peck in the grass,
six horses heads down in the green field.

Two guys in shadows brought the gurney,
wrapped his body in pale pink sheets,
as if once white and though washed
over and over, still held too much blood.

His couch carted off to the dump,
cigarette burns like bullet holes scattered
where his hand dropped—one ruined leather
couch, nothing compared to other things.

He never set his place on fire, too busy
to notice exit wounds in orbit in his prized
state of loss, tongue as sleek as mint varnish.

Like the Little Prince's beloved rose,
we loved him beyond all others, our prince,
now *Prince of Ash, Prince of What Could Have Been,*
the royal pity turns horses to ash, birds to stone.

Nothing of Plato at Lake Winnipeg

The lake was a lousy mirror where I wished
to find my reflection to determine if I was pretty—
the idea of my face, as Plato explains.

That's the way of teenage girls who look
for answers to unanswerable questions
while assessing the length of their hair.

After dinner while washing blue-and-white dishes,
the loud sound of crickets, the dog transfixed
by squirrels in motion up in the trees.

Nothing of Plato here, just Betty Crocker
stained with tomato sauce, annotated
recipes for tuna casserole and rhubarb pie.

My sister kept up about the neighbor boy.
Was he too old? Was his name Steward or Stewart?
Wasn't he the Scarecrow in the school play?

Her ponytail thick as a fist, how did she have so much hair?
We snuck another piece of pie, forks barely paused
gobbling it up over the Formica counter.

We stuck out purple tongues and laughed
so hard we had to bend over and hold our stomachs.
Are there better words to describe summer?

Now, a paradox—that sister is almost lost
in cards sent on holidays and birthdays,
messages left on voicemails back and forth.

Yet, the muddy lake-bottom remains clear
with the other essential Forms of summer—
the pail of berries, the pier in its marshmallow coat,

the adults out on the screened-in porch,
the slick ice in their gin-and-tonics,
these words to describe summer fail.

Cuts on my knee from going too fast
on my bike, Dad worked out the gravel,
the bathtub turned red. With a sturdy boy

by the enigmatic black basin of lake, the menthol
of his mouthwash harsh against my tongue.
When summer ended leaves raked in piles,

the lake resolved to hide its latent blue.
Plato wrote, *Death is not the worst thing.*
Earthen colors and smoothness of a thousand

pebbles collected all summer. How to choose
five to bring back to the city, as demanded?
Are there better words to describe winter?

On Being the Eldest

An older brother would offer protection,
explain that a *holding penalty* is worth
fifteen yards and give the inside scoop
on boys when they started to show up.

Instead, I taught my younger brother how to dance
to rock-and-roll in front of the mirror.
He laughed, shook his hair and kept the beat.
We once practiced kissing and never spoke of it again.

An older sister could pave the way,
impress teachers with her intelligence
before I showed up with lousy spelling,
explain tampons, term papers and first dates,
fix me up with a boy from her class who
otherwise would never have noticed me.

Instead, my little sister wouldn't talk.
The first day of middle school I had to tell
the ladies in hairnets behind the lunch counter
that she wanted the soup-and-sandwich special.
On the bus going home she whispered,
Tomorrow, I promise I'll talk.

Elegy for My Mother

My mother left specific instructions to be cremated,
her ashes strewn in the vineyard.
Right now I don't really care.
Her body lies in the Evergreen Mortuary on Geary.
Do they incinerate everyone all together once a day?
Does the attendant swallow a few Tums
before pulling on his rubber gloves?
Is KFOG playing pop tunes my mother would hate?

I can no longer call for her recipes, her trick
to keep the flourless chocolate cake from collapsing.
Things are striated, as if seen through fumes
of gasoline or the intense heat of a desert.

Tonight *Cavalleria Rusticana* will open
with Barbacini in the lead of Tiriddu.
Our seats on the end of row "M" will be empty,
we'll miss the plot to poison Pagliaccio and the duel.

For my tenth birthday she took me to Rigoletto.
I wore my velvet dress, she hummed the arias
under her breath and tapped her foot in time
to the music and I feel asleep, mesmerized
by the gold brocade on the seatback in front of me.
I tried to stay awake, to prove I was worthy.

On the Pediatric Ward

At the beginning of a story there is hope.
Nancy Blanchard's ponytail bounces in a circle
when she skips home for dinner.
Adam has not been out to play,
he has a "gene gone wrong,"
as Grandpa explains at the VFW over Pinochle.
Adam bangs his head on the kitchen floor,
chews his fingers deep to the bone,
stops breathing and turns blue, cannot stand
to be submerged in even a few inches of water.
Rob and Tilly have driven to Emergency at all hours,
using the short-cut behind the Old Fire Station
to avoid the slow light at Pettigrew, but
the only remedy is hidden in Rob's closet,
a bottle of Wild Turkey, always half-empty.
Adam's never looks directly at Sesame Street,
at their old white cat batting his feet,
at his red toothbrush in a plastic cup
labeled ADAM on adhesive tape,
he peers sideways, cowlick True North,
tapered hands in perpetual spin,
what's a Blanchard to do?
"Trust in God," says Minister Blackwell.
Adam sucks his fingers through prayers,
moans in falsetto while the congregation
robustly sings *Lamb of God*. The Neurologist,
new to town, has a Boston accent, wears
striped bow ties, prescribes tablets to be cut
in half that don't much help and a white helmet,
onto which Nancy smoothes her Batman sticker,
worrying Adam will not notice how brave
Batman looks, his hand aloft, astride his Bat Mobile.

More on the Death of My Brother

The finest mathematicians in Babylon and the physicist
from Princeton with a hole in the elbow of his sweater
disagree about the solution to the problem of zero.
Evidently this is a difficult problem, the mathematics of zero
is like death because the paradox remains unresolved.

This thing is divided into halves—how he could leave me
alone, and the other half—he never got to live in Chile,
steer his skiff out to fish the schools of snapper,
speak his Castilian Spanish to his one true love.

The concept of zero first appeared in the Year 628.
It does not add up, how can mathematicians claim
zero to be the sum of all numbers, how can something
be infinite and nothing, how can he be here and then he's not?

The sum of zero and a negative number is negative—
Does that mean I have forgiven him?
The sum of zero and a positive number is positive—
Does that mean my binary star is in heaven?
The sum of zero and zero is zero—
Does that mean none of it matters anyway?

This taunts me as I trudge up the hill to pay
the Evergreen Mortuary on Geary with my Visa,
they don't accept American Express, and to sign
the stack of papers required to authorize his cremation.

In the South End

Each year our Christmas walk took us away from the river
where well meaning people might bestow holiday greetings.
Rather, we walked south towards the old City Hospital,
along blocks of brownstones with an occasional flourish
of Victorian flamboyance in the cement flowers
carved over a double doorway or a wrought iron fence
plunged like small swords into the frozen earth.

We walked through deserted cobblestone streets
away from windows festooned with Christmas lights,
poinsettias and the swags of draperies in the frost
of our wasteland. Is it possible to find a better word,
one without echoes of Eliot, one that stands on its own
as a leafless oak waits for its deciduous genes
to untwist its dormant buds in the torrents of April?

We endured like a leash-less dog lost
in the woods, hungry as he forages,
peels of barking no one hears, that dog who
someone fondly named Henry or Merlin.
We mourned in silence each Christmas
the absence of children amid the gay
wrappings of our gifts, the hearth, cold,
the house, dog-less, the dinner table, set for two,
as we walked South, away from the light.

After Reading *Fear of Flying*

It started when he took me in his bed
and I realized I didn't want to be there.

This happened a few times before
I figured out it needn't happen again.

I could choose to leave a man who didn't care,
or actually some of them did, but I didn't

or couldn't. Penance at parties on stairwells
with cigarette, the laughter upstairs, down

in the dark taking turns with the bottle,
the butts, spasms of laughter, the banter

of nonsense or nearly nonsense, hair in a pony tail,
all of my face available—what an irony.

And sweater tight to show off, how did I manage that?
In the emergency room, a thick red hose

shoved down my throat, the doctor in yellow
gloves asks, *How many did you take?*

He pummels my shoulder, scolds, ugly tie
askew. So, I learned to leave, to practice

being someone else, give up kisses
for the tongue sensation, half-conscious

in sheets as the thrill declined, holding
something back that was mine—everything.

Vacation with Coal

It's late and unbelievably, someone begins
to practice a cello and plays Silent Night,
a strange ode in summer.

Why are the beds always too small,
the sheets so slippery, the soap so hard?
Unforsaken things that follow us to Truro,

we wrestle with tightly clamped shells
of bivalves that taste sweet, our feet buried
in wet sand, I've read this book before,

it's a parable about moving the cheese
or a spinster trapped in a town
that turns on her, transfixed as the evening

news repeats over and over—*the miners
are too deep to find.* Not to be self-absorbed,
but where are rescuers to unbind the cords

that tie us, unwind vows that sting
in the rough salt of this gray sea?
A bell sounds, six miners in Utah

no one can find, one thing is clear,
we will not return to Truro to rent
this weathered house again next year.

Robert *in Extremis*

He says it's logical to go ahead with cremation,
it will all be over fast.

He worries about bacteria breeding
under his skin, his hair nails curving they're so long.

It's not a pretty scene in the box.
Still, he's afraid—the crackle of his roasted face

his liver a molten yellow puddle.
He thinks of jumping of the roof—

a few more moments before eternity, without pain,
one last chance to contemplate gravity

doing its job to accelerate a falling mass.
It's irrational, he says, *I won't feel a thing.*

He bemoans their lies when they say, *It won't hurt a bit—*
before a flu shot, the dentist with a horse-sized needle

for the Novocain and surgery under the lights,
when you let them cut you open, do their work

and sew you back together while you listen
to their Brahms, Willie Nelson, the baseball game.

He hopes there's an anesthesia of afterlife
so potent he won't even notice when the pyre is lit.

Eileen on the Cancer Ward

Open the door, she will tell you about
her invaded left nipple, tossed
into an incinerator by hands
inside pale-yellow latex gloves,
seepage at the edge like the small pond
in the back yard, green with scum.

She might bring you herbs cut from her garden
tucked next to the house in a spot with morning sun.
Each afternoon off-balance on the shore road
out to The Light, she turns back after a short look
at the cove shining with boats.

Open the door, she can help you understand
the woman who stays home, the probability of genes
under the influence of too many cocktails
or not enough vegetables, who knows.
She counts to one instead of two.

She asks you what to do.
"Find the fruit stand with the best corn."
She knows what you mean—an open door,
enough to be unwhole in the summer
with peaches instead of bones.

With Ann Whose Husband Has PTSD

Once he stood tanned and muscled,
gulped a beer out on the pier
while a transistor blared rock'n'roll.

Hot sun, cold water, bait and tackle boxes,
all we knew was the fish, Northern Pike
we caught and fried up to eat with beer.

Now there's a tremor in his eyelid,
his hands fumble and he shakes
his head like a wet dog.

When he squeezes my shoulder,
he hope his fingers say something
he cannot. He's sick, he flails,

sleeps late, devours old comic books
collected when his giggle was famous
and his father called him, "Hi,"

short for hyena. She waits for him.
Like a snake molt, she watches for signs.
He's an animal she tries not to scare off.

She was nine when her father showed her
how to walk in the woods,
fawns so close she touched their mouths,

their breath moistened her hands,
the small mounds on their heads
that would grow into horns.

Betrayal

so sure of myself
thirty years ago in Cambridge
something stupid I did
after the Gary Snyder reading—
abandoning one man for another
without cause or at any rate
a good cause – something difficult
for something easy

riprap—to slow the frame
to tell a morality, a pureness
his bible of wilderness, not wildness—
soft stanza, soft stance

he builds a fence
brews tea, divides an apple with a sharp knife
hikes the ridge in the crease of heaven
at least so it seems

slanted eyes the wise color of water
baggy dark clothes whisper of Zen
wrinkled pixie face with the little beard
voice of rum

on folding metal chairs we rustled and coughed
electricity
we knew him or we thought we did
through his lines, a renegade from Reed
who crossed West to East and back
his tea cup empty
without mocking our tethers
a sensei, really
we could tell, the real thing

now I understand his powerful choices
to see through the dharma eye
every wondrous thing
able to blossom

a full circle
rereading *Riprap*
and my own choices
(ah, yes, alas that one was no good)
pen aloft
birds fly by
in formation

On Filing in Pima County

Superior Court Deputy Clerk 194 stamps our case number,
D43002756 in black on the *Petition for Dissolution of Marriage.*
The server goes down, but by the time he's finished stamping
all the pages, the lady in the next window yells over,
Hey, Gerald, we're up again. So, we walk out with final copies
on this final day before the clock starts the 60 days
after which, on day 61, we can go to court.
Twenty-six pages and a receipt for $387, we have to pay
extra to include our property settlementpursuant to
our *Marital Agreement,* which we ask the court to honor.
They say it will hit 103°. I get home and take a swim
and think about that clerk, a nice guy, he gave us a form
we were missing, *Affidavit Regarding Minor Children,*
apparently we need it though we never had kids.

Afraid to Keep a Gun

He can't tolerate kisses—
      though a peck on cheeks
      with a greeting he'll do.

The sex therapist explains,
      Sexual phobias may not be curable.

The smell puts him off, ruins
      compatibility of rolling
      a pie crust, tacking a wooden
      sailboat across Penobscot Bay,
      repainting the red barn.

No one could anticipate how fine the dissection
      of this "malignancy" would be required,
      not the psychoanalyst,
      not even *all* of psychoanalysis.
          (Freud himself,
          brought out of retirement, couldn't help.)
It deepens into a mystery
      classified under "irrevocable differences."

She bought a riding whip,
told him to hit her,
      a desperate act that led nowhere,
      no flame can burn in a vacuum.
Afraid to keep a gun,
      he explained it to her once.

But the little flame is out. Out, out.
That sound!—Out.
      It all throws him off.

(Everyone knows, if a rider is thrown,
he must get back on right away.)

The verdict is in, the jury pronounces *injury*,
first degree, full thickness,
nothing a tissue can sop up.

So, she leaves
with only suitcases filled with cotton, velvet, linen,
goose feathers—soft things to wrap around her body.

A New Appreciation for
Liz Taylor & Eddie Fisher

Certain things were evident or should have been
because Eddie required total darkness when he slept,
whereas, Liz craved fresh air though the open window—
an impasse that might seem unimportant, but examined
closely on an evening when the caress of April in the breeze
could drive one crazy and became the fulcrum on which rests
the fate of things bigger than marriage, for example, the fate
of a huge marble slab from Fantiscritti, a quarry
on the slopes of Mount Maggiore northeast of Carrara,
whether it might crack into shards under the onslaught
of M's chisel or peel back its veins to reveal
the magnificent form of David despite its flaw,
the sort of "either-or" equation that becomes unsolvable,
despite their fondest wish to attain *music of the spheres.*

On Moving Across the Country to Get a Divorce

1.
In Jamaica beads cling to beer bottles,
shells flaunt coral music, but he will not go in the water!
Pale legs crossed on the chaise,
he reads psychoanalysis and frowns.

His curlicue notes in black fountain pen dipped in the ink jar
without a spill, dipped once, twice, she's lost count.
Locked fireproof filing cabinets with secrets he will take to
        his grave.
Rooty-toot-toot, off to the Institute,
Boston has two psychoanalytic institutes,
in August the Truro beaches are full of shrinks.

He sits under the eaves in the shade
with his pipe and his smoky Earl Gray tea,
When is a pipe just a pipe?
His size 13 chukkas by the potbellied stove,
bridges named for fallen Harvard warriors,
the ice between them, unplumbed—
talk doesn't always heal, of this she is sure, Dr. Freud.

2.
She paints her room blue, by the blue sea
under a blue sky on the Left Coast,
the refuge of pioneers looking for a better life.
A good loss, can that be said?
Well-deserved tears are not shed.
Secrets though respected, are not precious,
blue is precious and the difference, 3000 miles, incalculable.

Opposite Magnetic Poles

Attracted to the light and the dark,
to choose would kill me.

With open legs I am just another
furred creature, which reminds me

of the three baby quails abandoned
after weeks of rain, their mother

tucked her head down in the miserable cold,
left after all her work and it was impossible

to check on them anymore, look into their eyes,
watch them stop hopping and curl up

into balls against the cold, for a day
they slept and then I wrapped their remains

in a paper towel to throw away,
two hands that clap between movements

when you should wait until the end
to applaud, some oboe player grimaces

at those enthusiastic few who do not know
better and that is the problem, I never know

better, open legs so a new generation
of innocents will follow into the dirty air

that makes sunsets more beautiful.
Have you got any better ideas?

The Shade of My Father

I ask what it's like to be old.
Just leave the barn door open,
even old horses can find their way
by the scent of the hay.

He yells, *Our senators are sissy,*
pansy double-talkers. Don't fight
a war if you aren't willing to do what it takes
to win. He reminds us he's been to war,
the jungle ate his socks and when the bomb
was dropped, he was relieved,
maybe he could get home, after all.

I wait for it to drop, news will come
when I'm asleep, bathing, paying bills,
in the yard, under the eaves, in the root cellar,
empty wooden bins with only the scent of apples.

He will be alone in a box, not even his dog
to keep him company, no pharaoh,
he won't be buried with his wife, his soldiers,
his coins, even his legions of wisdom will evaporate,
no more stories, his mind will turn to brain.

Trapped in a hotel elevator, he told us about,
those Woolworth brothers, the kingpins
of five-and-dimes who borrowed $300 and invented
a whole new way to shop, not a sales clerk
in the whole damn store—we forgot to be thirsty.

Worried about the sunfish, how they turned gray
on the stringer, he bellowed,
God put the sunfish in the lake for us to eat!

He parted the sea, but in the end, no more
than any man, it's coming like a slap,
everyday older, a warrior asleep over his reading,
the dog chews his crown fallen to the ground.

His ears fill with crickets, no memory of names,
the score, our birthdays, his anniversary,
this man who will end in me and exceed
himself through me—half my alphabet of braided
protein machinery, well-made, well-honored.

What Melissa Told Me on the Locked Ward

There's a voice in her head,
or maybe not. A white bird
doesn't tell her what to do
or anything like that. And a red bird.
Sometimes things go quiet for months.

Inside the bull's liquid eye wings flap,
she's warned about the shower, the razor blade.
My father killed himself, you know.
Another white bird, just over there.
Do you have a light?

She pinches her arm, sometimes a singe,
just a little circle, as round as their beady eyes,
It doesn't hurt, you know.

In the morning before the noise starts up,
when light is slanted, she sees that green bird,
she never sees a yellow bird.
Water changes color in weather, you know.
She smokes *Benny Henny's*, but prefers Kools.

On the front page she sees a little girl
somewhere in Africa, left behind in the sand,
She's starving, you know.
Her head is too big. It's no good,
see that big vulture beside her.
See that bird over there?
That is a dangerous bird.

At the Pearly Gates

You might think death's door would be choked
    with the rasp of meat-eating birds,
but would you imagine a crown of doves,
    sudden weightlessness, unbound from myocardial
demands to squeeze sixty times a minute,
    blessed escape from imperious dominion
of the white sponge of brain, stores of worry,
    scurry of minions, legions who work
the pedals of its wheel around, unleashed from weight—
    of bones, thighs, hunger—for coffee, whiskey,
sleep, desire to watch fireflies,
    chat with neighbors, chew on, say, licorice
or malt balls, released from endorphins, adrenaline,
    arrow heads, self-seal envelopes, umbrellas,
all of it—forsaken as surely as a spaceship exits
    earth's atmosphere, the familiar erased,
in an ever-lasting peace, mitochondria set free
    from their preoccupation with ATP,
glucose phosphorylation, adrift from the currency
    of carbon transfer, beyond ambitions
of twin bellows, galley slaves who row
    back-and-forth to move air in-and-out
twelve times a minute, from the demands of a bladder,
    emancipated from the curse of oxygen,
blue as it falls off its hemoglobin horse,
    from labor and pain—of bone on bone,
warts, hemorrhoids, cracked teeth, the onset of —
    eternity's surprise luxury—to unfurl,
unwind, uncoil DNA, uncrimp proteins,
    disconnect axons, shoot off fireworks
of a body finally in eternal rest.

Dinnertime at the Hana Kai Maui Hotel

Too embarrassed to look at him when he could not look back,
Mom said, *He's still handsome,* her hand in his hair.

When the rain is not water swallow me whole.
No, wait, I've changed my mind, spit me out.

His skin already so cool, a bit yellow, hands open,
tobacco-stained fingers, head tilted back—I'm nauseated.

The armies of the hills swarm down to take the docks.

A long-tailed yaeger flies low over the cupid waves
hunting for dinner, I cannot eat when the rain is not water.

The armies pour hot oil over the walls.

I am not hungry, who can eat a cow?
I think I'll drink my way through, one careful glass at a time.

To Wash Sand

Tell me what you do all those evenings
when you say you do nothing.

I don't remember placing snapdragons
from my nosegay here inside pages
of the fat e.e. cummings collected poems.

It's a farce, I play the jilted wife,
impossible to wash out the stain of sea,
more acidic near the mouth of the estuary.
I might or might not smile at the children
who play on the shore—it depends.

Are you tired of me or of yourself?

Holding hands through a rain of rice,
vows slip through our fingers.
We don't just live together, the stakes are much higher.

At Il Forno with friends you smile,
your hand on Vera's shoulder,
how she expands in your focus.
I see how she blossoms.

Over the breakfast table your eyes are discs
blanched of light and my damn coffee
isn't hot and spills a little when I bring the cup
to my lips—my lips, your ruined napkin left behind.

The lady in Portugal darned lace on her balcony,
her calloused fingers quicker than the eye could follow—
that village where we were happy.

On your heels you rocked back and forth,
studying the glint of her needle.
Your smile opens inward.
I couldn't see that then, how it opens inward.

When the cockatiel was a baby, pale yellow
burrowed in my hands. Now he sits, head cocked.
Does he know? Can a bird know?
I make dinner, shape the patties, mold the meat
to segue to our next chapter whose title might be *rediscovery,*
resume, redeem, recover, regain, rescue, revive.
Rrrrrrr........from the bird.
I pull out seeds out of the lemon.
Rrrrrrrrrrr...

The Bright Light

Oliver Sacks wrote about a man struck by lightning,
near-dead, surrounded by bright light—
now he's different, obsessed with classical music.
On scans, parts of his brain light up, an alteration.

When my mother was near-dead,
her numbers were lousy—
blood pressure, cardiac output, oxygen saturation—
everything marginal, in a plane we cannot see,
where beings exist like the corners of stars
beyond the calculations of astronomers,
certainly beyond the ken of a respiratory therapist
who adjusts the settings of her respirator.
No, this has nothing to do with karma,
reincarnation, serial lives with the unremembered
promise of progress, from flea to cow to Buddha.
Something less linear, something impossible
to describe except maybe in the equations of physics.

I whispered for her to come back,
told her we needed her *here*, to be courageous.
I told her that a few times,
although I wasn't sure if that was the right word,
couldn't imagine what it might mean to a star
in a different universe, disconnected from the *woosh*
of her ventilator, hovering just-beyond my touch,
her skin hot and dry.

Now, she says she remembers nothing,
just that it was awful, so awful she prefers
not to discuss it. I can tell there are things
she hasn't said and a few times
she's mentioned the light, although she's not sure.

With Vicky
Whose Husband Died of Leukemia

In the rainy season she pressed against the bottom of the tub,
they rode in a rickshaw through back streets and argued.

They made up in a cheap hotel room,
the chenille bedspread left marks on her back.

In the rainy season blood like jelly swirled
into an underworld river, their baby lost.

The rainy season just over when he needed
Boston's supply of platelets, every last little bag.

He looked inscrutable, anything she had was worthless,
then he become the god of rain.

She visited him beneath his stone,
when the rain ruined the flowers, she didn't care.

The Locked Ward: Death Flowers
(first red then white)

Their botanical name is a mouthful,
papaver somniferum, red flowers of joy.

Please fix yourself, Mrs. Williamson.
H, junk, dust, skag—white slavery
in a $30 bag of fool's gold.
Nothing softens the blow
of such sclerotic snow
that smacks you into kamikaze
dives you explain with lies that ricochet.

Blizzards cloak the cornfields of Ohio
where remission is twelve steps away.
A dismal halfway house, your unruined soprano
sings The Supremes and Dolly Parton as your
feet shuffle and you snap your fingers.

"Doc, are you friend or foe?"
I answer, "Maybe half of both."

At the church, I stand by Shawnelle
who you liked best, friends dazed
at the buffet, stories of your better days.
No savior could thwart you—shoveled
effaced into earth's cellar,
spiderlily, jasmine and dodder.

When The Weather Hits

1.
We study *apoptosis* of cells to understand
why ... babies get brain cancer.

And dreams? Even Freud couldn't explain—
paradoxical sleep or finger painting?

And exhaustion, what is that molecule,
too little of something, too much, or both?
Whatever it is, it's present at dawn
when they call because the heartbeat is gone,
the Death Certificate must be signed.

2.
A man crashed his rig, his hand
immobilized, wired like a harp.

His wife ironed by the window,
a speeding van ran over their son
whose ball bounced into the Parkway.

Her broken heart sets off our bells,
he paces cradling his forearm,
she hears angels, she says they're singing
up near the top of her window—
we up her dopamine.

3.
We sit in the eye of the body's weather.
Some guy can't stop hiccupping—
from the Latin, *singult: to catch ones breath
while sobbing,* a lady without hair is caught
revolving in the door, parents cry against the glass.

We scribe the fevers, the falls, counts, lacunae
like monks, we fulfill our oaths as the weather hits.

Time Traveler

On my way to meet my mother at the Poiret exhibit,
I walk through the enormous hall when out of the corner
of my eye I see my husband standing twelve feet tall,
motionless, gorgeous in white marble, his gaze steady
across the vast Greek and Roman collection of the Met.
I stop stunned, but then I've seen him in the most unlikely places—
in a 14th Century Flemish woodcut of a boat with red bearded
rowers on their way to battle or lounging on the floor
of the Medici Chapel, an olive branch in his three-foot hand,
on a black horse galloping, lance level, visor drawn.
Where will I see him next, tossing mail on the counter,
bemoaning how his serve let him down in the second set,
fridge open to find a bottle of Coors, in this life, mine for a few
decades during the centuries where he travels in various guises?

Underwater in Belize

Underwater above the reef, he looked different—
skin tinged salmon-pink, eyes distorted, wide
behind his goggles, and yet what I am trying
to describe had nothing to do with his body.
We were meeting as if for the first time in the frolic
of that underwater school of blue moon fish, so close
we could touch them and yet we were more wondrous
than even the carpet of purple coral that waved,
the small school sharks who ignored us, or at least,
that's how it felt as we swam close together.
And what now, midway in our marriage?
The magic of that swim has not diminished.
I go back there when I feel lost to enjoy
the pinks, the bubbles and the sparkles.

Pamela Needs a Higher Dose of Zoloft

She listens to her dead parents through the keyhole—
She's lost, what are they talking about?
She opens the door to an empty room,
rain streaming down the windows.
Empty rooms make her dizzy.
Did she take her pill?
Yes, she clearly recalls the blue tablet
shaped like a football in her cupped
palm, down at the tap mouth against metal,
water into her mouth. So, why does she hear them?

They talk to each other as her mother sets
the table with two forks on each napkin,
a dinner fork, a salad fork.
Her dad explains risk, *it's part
of every investment, you've got
to have the stomach for it.*
She is not making this up.

The early rains ruin the grapes,
the dog chases rabbits and squirrels
down by the creek, wine glasses
are washed by hand, the flue is difficult
to open, they pull the skiff high on the beach
each winter—she remembers everything.
She was not the right child—that boy
came too-early the year before she was born.

When He Went to Ground

My parents decide not to hire someone
to find him, we just have to wait.
Stupid to buy a ticket with a connection
in Vegas, that was tempting fate.
My mother and I chat about nothing
so often I lose count. What is he doing?
Is he alive? What are we doing?

The wine glass shatters on the Saltillo,
freight trains up from Mexico toot
as they brake against the track.
I am not on a train, he is not on a train.
Why am I not completely clear?
I am not on a train, he is not on a train.

My husband uses the skimmer to throw
frogs over the fence out onto the street,
he sets rat traps with peanut butter for bait.
I sit out on the banco in the heat,
the monsoon roils in over the Santa Ritas,
tortoises pile up on the fallen Mesquite.
I dare the lightening to hit me, I dare it.

Morocco

I dip my toe into Africa and it comes out
black, smeared with the dung of donkeys,
harassed by hustlers, bargained down to dust,
filled with tagines and stench of rotten fruit.

I dip my toe into Africa and it comes out
inspired by Arab Spring, thirsty, callous
to beggars, impervious to calls for prayer,
overpowered by the weak and the strong.

I dip my toe into Africa and it's bitten off,
spat upon, carried by throngs in the Souk,
tattooed in Henna, on the verge of tears,
poorer yet richer, I am missing more than a toe.

I dip my toe into Africa and fall in love
with djembe drums, slippers with pointy toes,
Berber carpets, rooftop gardens, Tuareg jazz,
mosaics, storks with nests on streetlamps.

I dip my toe into Africa and begin to drown,
sucked into quicksand, poisoned by the bite
of a snake, stolen into the desert and hidden
among veiled women who whisper evil omens.

I dip my toe into Africa and lose my cash.
See, dogs here don't bark,
except the tiny ones on leash,
so many stray kittens, not many cats.

Matter

I would like to give you this CD of Tuareg
jazz I brought back from Marrakech.

I would like to stop visiting your old driveway
to stare at your front door while I sit in my car.

If you were here, we could discuss my latest fury
at Mom because she does not like my poems,

especially the ones about you she insists
are for my own notoriety rather than

my way to skirt the landmines you put in my path.
You know, fatal ones like your Stage IV demise.

You would like these songs, the heavy rhythm
of the Bodhran drum offset by the lilt of the Kora.

I can see you nod to the beat as we drink Snapple
out on your balcony and watch the oranges fall.

I'm sure we'd talk about things that matter
along the zip line that runs between us.

Things We Said Today

He's up there singing duets with Marvin,
on air guitar with Al Green, down with Lennon
while he chops onions and chorizo for paella.
He says, "yum yum" over and over as he eats
the sweetest meat of the claw, has an "ah ha"
moment when he apprehends *approach avoidance*,
cries when Achilles loans his armor to Patroclus.
He slides on black ice, picks up hitch hikers,
runs late for appointments, forgets to get a hair cut,
at meetings never fails to toss a few bucks
into the coffee can. He reads the wind when
he fishes for Blues, dances across the bow
to drop anchor, squints into the sun to find
the gulls swoop into the chop, reliable harbingers
of fish he'll clean while he hums a bit of Handel.

In the Basement

The first day of anatomy class we were reminded
to respect the bodies, warned not to pull any pranks.

When we pulled back the plastic, the cadavers
were yellow and swollen like wooden anchors

of their former selves left too long underwater
with deepfreeze injected into their veins.

Their fat was slabs of golden curds, their muscles
shred, nothing was as it should be, particularly

the pointless memorization of the branches
off the facial artery and the bones of the foot.

The dead weight of their legs brought visions
of the drowned and soldiers on gurneys

back from the trenches with soiled bandages
wrapped around their foreheads and glazed eyes.

The smell of formaldehyde drove us into the hall,
to tales of men found inside the stomach of whales.

Though we wore gloves, our hands reeked,
each day we threw our clothes into the laundry.

Janet fainted when she peeked inside the sawed open skull
of her lady and found a brain with so many holes

it looked like a kitchen sponge with an enormous clot
in Broca's area where we'd learned language resides.

Tales of a Science Correspondent

1.
Barrow, 320 miles above the Arctic Circle is
the cloudiest place on earth—Inupiat
eat seals, walrus, caribou, ugruk, whale
duck, ptarmigan, fish, polar bear and candy.

Understatement is always best, though tough
when exploding harpoons send up geysers
of steam from whale innards and the liver's
lining is carried off like a cape by the eldest
boy to make a drum and buzz saws carve
slabs of *muktuk* in the stench of red snow.

January moon of the returning sun, *siqinyasaq
Tatqi*, September moon when birds fly south,
December moon with no sun and winter's White
Dwarf lies lost below the horizon of Polar Night.

Alaska's thin sea ice and shrinking hares
mule deer, beetles, pocket gophers, diatoms—
things start to fall apart, a solitary polar bear
adrift brings back a memory of being lost
in scrub oak without a compass, at last
traffic noise miles off led me to a road.

2.
A Golden Gate toll attendant shaken up
by four guys in a blue Prius that sped off
after she was handed four dollar bills folded
in a hand that smelled of formaldehyde and felt
like a dead fish, the Dean bemoaned how
this prank might derail donations of cadavers,

which I didn't use and thankfully no eager
editor demanded a photo of the ghoulish hand.

3.
Astronomers postulate unstable binary stars
detonate into Supernovae with more energy
than our Sun over its life of ten billion years,
double stars so dense, a teaspoon would weigh
over a ton and blow helium wind storms towards
its twin, setting off a thermonuclear explosion
that forms a neutron star—Andy was my binary
star, but he died before we could blast off
to bring forth a star I'd have named Salvation
because if we'd exploded his ashes would not
lie tossed between rows of Cabernet Sauvignon
in my parents' vineyard that abuts Conn Creek.

Sunday Night Emergency Room

I pick up the chart and walk in to an unwell
skinny guy with tell-tale KS on cheek and chin.
My gut hurts bad, a blade's inside, gotta help me, doc,
it's real bad—his fist indents his stomach and twists

before he snaps down his embroidered jeans
too low for me—scaphoid belly, blue snake,
pierced navel, strawberry pubic hair shaved
below his flaccid penis a curved worm.

I bolt outside and shut the door, fast breaths
without much air, then back inside I scold softly
cover him with a paper exam sheet, palpate
a weird mass like nothing I've ever felt before.

His KUB on the light-box—a mouse hunkers
down inside his transverse colon, perfect little
rodent skeleton huddled inside the man's gut,
he admits to a *sex game* out of my realm.

I page Surgery and explain why my patient
needs an emergency laparotomy to extract
a mouse that may be dead or alive—
silence, I have to explain it twice.

Chopin's Collar

To be placed in the Time Capsule
along with the mobile phone, a packet

of birth control pills and bark
from an Algonquin "long nose" canoe—

to hold the whole, more than the sum
of its parts—would these artifacts

tell extraterrestrial archeologists more
about us than a poem? I cut this bulb of anise

with a serrated knife, women tote water from the well.
Water trickles between fingers, lost.

That's where this is going, disappearance—
of water, of things besides the thin skins

of cucumbers tossed away. Arpeggios run
about as tomatoes are sliced, juice spills

onto the cutting board. Tall cattle herders
with bandoliers slung across their chests

drink blood from gourds, fathers
are shot or dropped down wells—

a knob is turned up too high.
Puree cilantro in the blender with olive oil,

lemon juice, salt and pepper.
One of the guests will probably hate the taste

of cilantro—its bright green, beautiful against
the flesh of the tomatoes, the tongues

of endive and, most of all, the curls of lettuce
like the furls of Chopin's infamous dress collar,

the polyphony of his *Fantasie in F minor* contrapuntal
to war orphans and the whirr of the blender.

Acknowledgements

To my teachers, especially David O'Neill who first brought poetry into the classroom. Oh, for an Irish accent to read Dylan Thomas. To Marvin Bram, at Hobart, who taught so many how to enter the world of ideas. To The Francis W. Parker School in Chicago for teaching their students how to learn. Thank you to The Poetry Center of the University of Arizona for their contribution to the greater writing community in Tucson. And for my teachers, especially: Paul Muldoon, Tony Hoagland, Dean Young and Robert Wrigley.

A very special thanks to Mindy F. Schirn and Jenifer Clement for their generous help with my writing over many years.

In recognition of grandparents, my family of origin and my husband, Mark Vibbard—the highs and lows of tough love.

To the editors of *JAMA, New Works Review, Moon Journal, The Journal of Medical Humanities, Cutthroat* for poems that have been re-titled and/or appear in a different version in this manuscript. 'Remembering Thee Walled Cemeteries' appears in the 2011 Anthology printed by *Arsenic Lobster.* The poem 'Amsterdam' won the 2008 Faulkner Prize for Poetry. Poems in this book have been shortlisted for the *Black Lawrence Poetry Book Award* and the *Hippocrates Prize for Poetry & Medicine,* 'An Air Flight from Rio to Paris' was a finalist for the Joy Harjo Contest. The author won the 2012 W.D. Snodgrass Fellowship.

And lastly to my brother, my lost binary star.

CPSIA information can be obtained at www.ICGtesting.com
Printed in the USA
LVOW060110080312

272018LV00008B/18/P

9 781848 611979